4/08

How to Draw

Independence Day
Things

For Jesse, Jasmine, Justin, Jordan, Melina, and Matthew

Published in the United States of America by The Child's World®
1980 Lookout Drive • Mankato, MN 56003-1705
800-599-READ • www.childsworld.com

Acknowledgments
Illustration and Design: Rob Court
Production: The Creative Spark, San Juan Capistrano, CA

Registration

Library of Congress Cataloging-in-Publication Data
Court, Rob, 1956–
  How to draw Independence Day things / by Rob Court.
    p. cm. — (Doodle books)
  ISBN 978-1-59296-954-8 (library bound : alk. paper)
  1. United States—In art—Juvenile literature. 2. Emblems in art—Juvenile literature. 3. Drawing—Technique—Juvenile literature.
4. Fourth of July celebrations—Juvenile literature. I. Title. II. Series.

NC825.U55C68 2008
743'.893942634—dc22

2007013392

The Scribbles Institute™

Doodle BOOKS ™

How to Draw

Independence Day Things

by Rob Court

The Child's World®

sky rocket

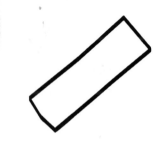

1

2

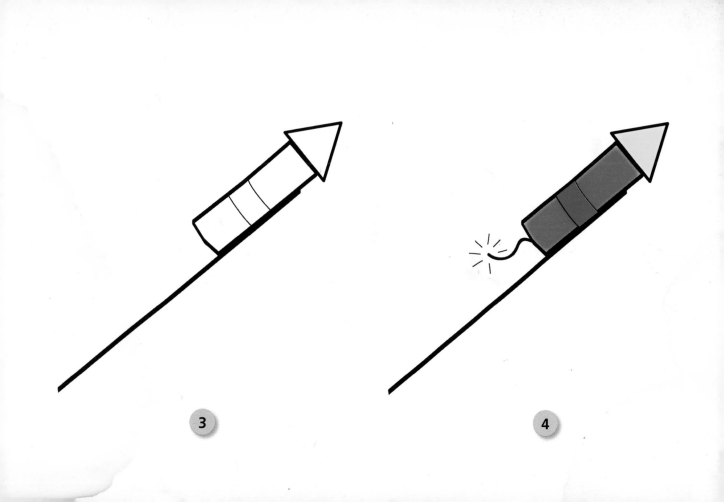

3

4

Washington Monument

1

2

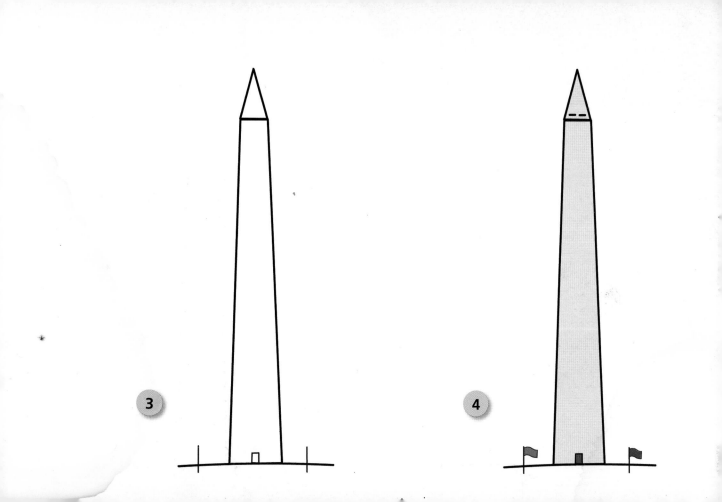

watermelon

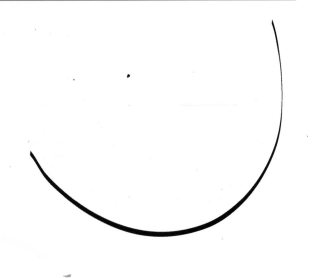

3

4

apple pie

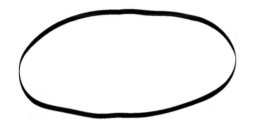

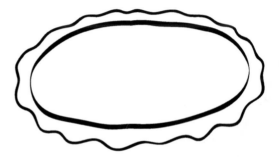

1

2

3

4

sparkler

1

2

3

4

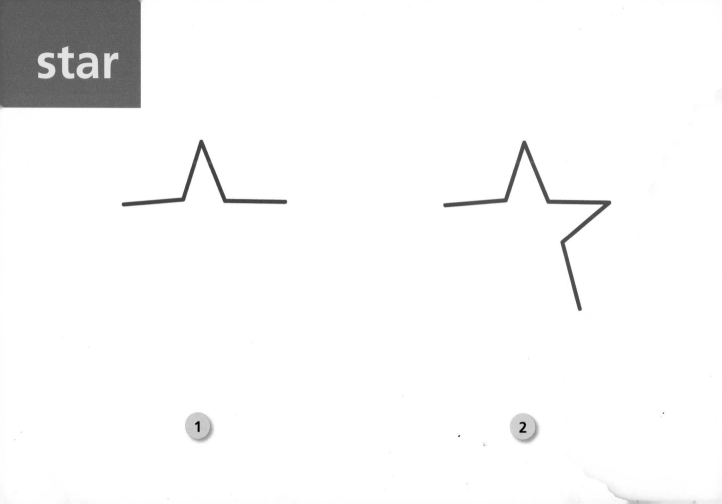

star

1

2

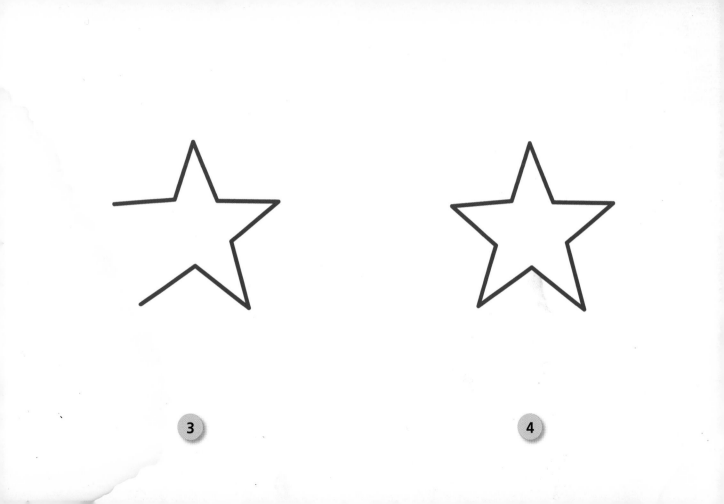

3

4

American flag

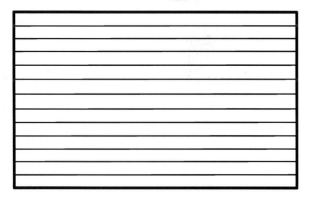

1

2

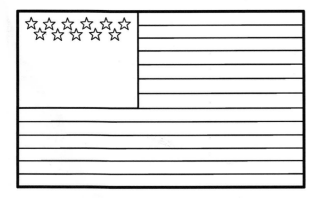

3

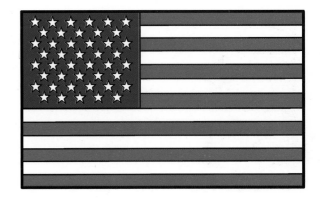

4

1

2

3

4

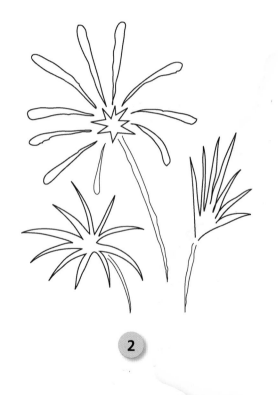

1

2

3

4

1

2

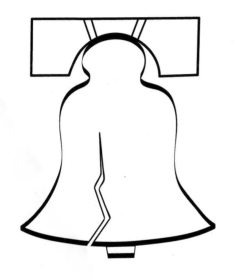

3

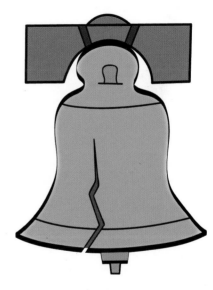

4

1

2

3

4

White House

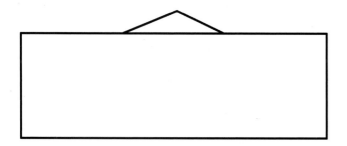

1

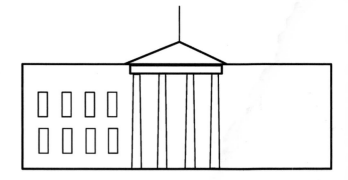

2

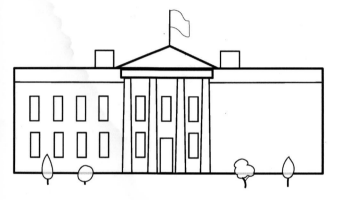

3

4

Statue of Liberty

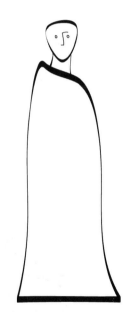

1

2

3

4

Mount Rushmore

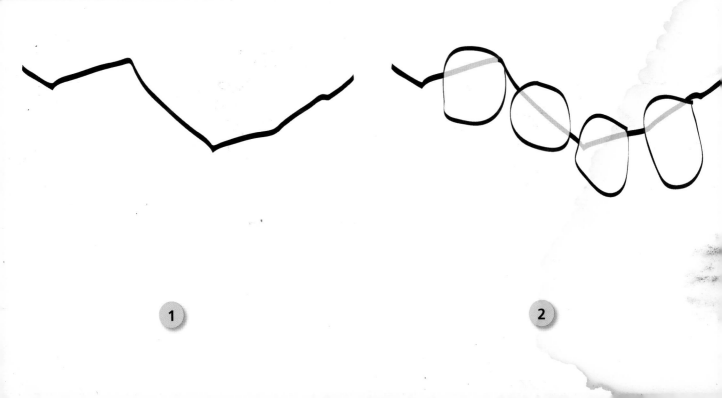

lines

horizontal

vertical

angled

curved

thick

thin

dotted

point

Move a point to make a line.

Connect lines to make a shape.

Shapes make all kinds of wonderful things!

squiggly

dashed

loop

Repeating dots, lines, and shapes makes patterns.

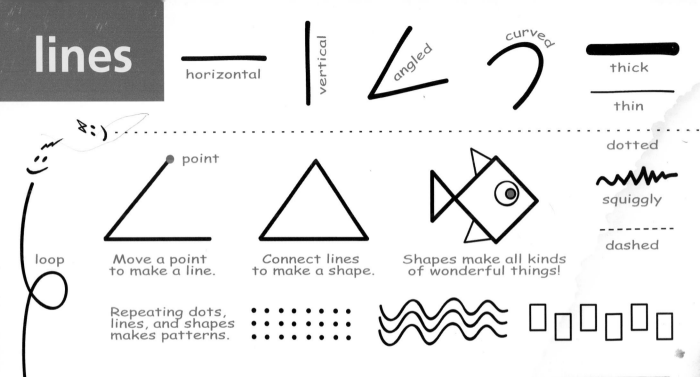

About the Author

Rob Court is a graphic artist and illustrator. He started the Scribbles Institute to help students, parents, and teachers learn about drawing and visual art. Please visit www.scribblesinstitute.com